Working Cats

Working Cats

BY TERRY DEROY GRUBER

J. B. Lippincott Company   New York

Designed by Abigail Moseley

U.S. Library of Congress Cataloging in Publication Data
Main entry under title:
Working cats.
   Includes index.
   1. Cats—Pictorial works. I. Gruber, Terry deRoy.
SF446.W67   779'.32   79-15991
ISBN 0-397-01376-0   80 81 82 83 84 10 9 8 7 6 5 4 3 2 1
ISBN 0-690-01951-3 pbk.   80 81 82 83 84 10 9 8 7 6 5 4 3 2 1

To Anne

For all your love, honesty, wisdom, and encouragement

Acknowledgments

I would like to thank the following people for their contributions to *Working Cats.*

Larry Ashmead, my editor, for his faith, good judgment, and guidance throughout the project.

Melissa Patenaude and Wendy Olson, my assistants, whose commitment, efficiency, and imagination were essential to the finished product.

Steven Kaufmann for his thoughtfulness in recommending me to the publishers.

Brian Cox, Lippincott's man behind the scenes, for his extra, extra editorial efforts.

Steven Fischer (the fish that saved Pittsburgh), for diamond ideas and a voice of reason.

Mike Gardere, for a thousand work prints on a small budget in record time.

Mike Levins, for his excellent final prints.

Jamie deRoy for her inspiration and her cats, my roommates and practice models.

Bill Hayward, for his resources and referrals.

Lisa Greene, for her scheduling of the final shootings.

Diane Saxe, for her patient and sensitive art direction.

Gai Moseley, for transforming mere pictures and words into a work of art.

And my good friends and acquaintances who provided the sound words, advice, and opinions that were so helpful:

Aaronel deRoy Gruber, Alexander Guest, Charlie Wagner, Gwen Wattenberg, Jeff Wilmot, Paul Wilmot, Cora Wen, Peter Oliver, Vanessa Murphy, Sandy Glorian, Susan Moskowitz, Miles Chapin, Anne Dayton, Jane Kleinman, Rich Lynch, J. C. Suares.

My appreciation is extended to the following institutions: Nikon Professional Services, Marty Forsher Professional Camera Repair, The American Society of Magazine Photographers, the Society of Photographer and Artist Representatives, the ASPCA, the Humane Society, and the U.S. Army.

Of course, my deepest gratitude and special thanks go to all the participants—cat owners, cat lovers, cat spotters—who took the time to answer our needs and accommodate our shootings.

Last, but not least, thank you Talese for adopting me, making me a cat lover and a "working person."

Introduction

There are cats who laze around the house content to let the world pass them by. And then there are cats who want more out of life than two sure meals a day and a fresh box of kitty litter. They are tough cats, street-wise cats, cats that bring home the bacon other cats are content to eat. They are cats that have found a comfortable niche in the workday world as mousers, mascots, watchcats, window displays, and, of course, table waiters. These are the Working Cats. And this book is full of them.

Giselle

Pet Shop

It must be every cat's dream to live in a pet shop.

Customer

Percy

Café

Sometimes Percy's tail gets in the way of a customer and he lets out a yelp. He knows that's one of the risks we run in the restaurant business—losing our tails.

Owner

Hamlet

The Algonquin Hotel

The writers who come in here gab too much. They could learn something about deep thought from Hamlet.

Waiter

Pete

Classic Cars Showroom

Pete has illusions of great wealth and grandeur. He's the classiest cat I know. But like some rich people he's very timid and lonely.

Salesman

16

Gina

Smoke/News Shop

No change without purchase!

Sign on cash register

18

Joanna

Secondhand Furniture Store

Joanna sits on a cushion all day like a little princess. Always perfectly poised and composed.

Refinisher

Brandy

Liquor Store

Brandy? We only named her that because of her color.

Store Owner

Slugger

Stadium

Slugger spent the entire winter on waivers. During the season he'll be a free agent on my grounds crew. He'll be working for no money, just room and board—and all the popcorn, peanuts and hot dogs he can eat.

Grounds Keeper

Stella

Shoe Store

Stella fits perfectly into a men's size 12.

Store Owner

Fuzzy

Fish Market

I found Fuzzy sixteen years ago on the street when she was a kitten. We fed her with an eyedropper and raised her right alongside our dog. Given a choice, she'll go for a salmon over a tilefish any day. Class.

Store Owner

Eagle, Birdie, and Bogey

Golf Course

They just showed up one day. I think they stay in the shelter next to the thirteenth tee. I was amazed they could survive the winter. No one owns them, no one feeds them. I've only gotten about ten feet from them before they tear off.

They've certainly made my job a lot easier. Since they arrived they've scared off all the gophers. I just wish they'd do something about all the golfers.

Grounds Keeper

Stray

All a stray cat does is struggle to survive.

Animal Control Warden

Heckle and Jeckle

Kindergarten

I'm the one in this classroom with the college degree, but
sometimes I think Heckle and Jeckle have more common
sense. They seem to know what kids are thinking and feeling.
When the kids are down, the two of them really turn into
clowns. It helps to pick things up.

Kindergarten Teacher

John-John

Botanical Gardens

We think John-John was born here at the Botanical Gardens. One day about four years ago John-John walked into my office. He had a bad infection which cost $50 to clear up, so I put up a sign and we collected $125. Now he has a bank account and it's worth over $500. He's registered with personnel as a Rodent Control Officer.

Secretary

Morris

Racetrack

Cats are smart. We make horses
and dogs run for our own
entertainment. But did you ever
hear of a cat race? Or a cat-
drawn carriage? No way. They've
got a mind of their own.

Horse Trainer

41

Max

Art Gallery

The art business is a lot like the pet business. If you find something you like, it will give you years of pleasure.

Gallery Director

Clyde

Lutheran Church

We had a cat for nine years named Luther. He found his way into the church Christmas Eve 1969 and never attempted to leave. He died last September. This Christmas Clyde appeared, homeless and hungry. You can see he isn't looking for another place of worship.

Deacon

Chi Chi

Bodega

Chi Chi is a working cat because he eats mice, and him being here means we have no rats.

Grocer

49

Prince Harry

Handbag Store

Since Harry came on board our staff has grown—we now have a cleaning woman.

Store Owner

Daisy

Flower Shop

The best story about Daisy is the time I had a nativity scene in the window. Daisy just pulled the baby Jesus out of the manger and slept there herself.

Florist

Puff, Omar, Tiki, and Sebrina

Show Biz

Who says you can't teach old cats new tricks?

Puff is the lead cat. Omar, Tiki, and Sebrina are the copycats. Puff taught the others to get on and off the bike, and how to roll over and sit. So when I say "Central Park" all the cats get onto their bikes.

The gang is really a hardworking bunch. They've done three books for beginning readers. They've been on the news. And they're always picking up a few dollars in the park on weekends. They were even voted the second most popular animals in New York—second only to Patty Cake the gorilla.

Cat Trainer

56

Pinocchio

Puppeteer's Studio

Pinocchio gets very jealous of my marionettes. He's destroyed several. I've tried telling him he'd hate having all those strings attached.

Puppeteer

59

Stanley

Cat Show

Now Stanley here is a hard worker. It's tough modeling all day and traveling all over the country. But he's a beauty and he knows what he's doing.

Cat Show Judge

Diablo, Tyme, Shano, Sascha

and GiCo the dog

Voice Studio

All our animals are music lovers.... When I teach, the student
has the advantage of singing to a captive audience.

Voice Instructor

63

Ken Cat

Lingerie Boutique

I will never wear out Ken Cat.

Boutique Owner

Vanilla

Soda Fountain

We've got a special fountain drink named after old Vanilla. It's a vanilla Coke. We call it a Cat-a-tonic.

Soda Jerk

66

Simon

Library

Simon's a thinking man's cat. After a hard day on the job he's likely to curl up in the 100s—that's philosophy, of course.

Librarian

73

Jennie

Grocery Store

I was over on aisle B with the household supplies. Something was funny but I wasn't really paying attention. I'd just finished stamping prices and reached up and started stocking and *whap!* The little monster nailed me.

Stock Boy

Ora

Calligraphy and Illumination Studio

Ora likes to make impressions. Unfortunately, her cat-apostrophes are major cat-astrophes.

Calligrapher

Tiger, Lionelle, and Frosty

Stationery Store

The first time I saw Frosty she was pregnant. She showed up on my doorstep one day and by the next day there were nine more. I love them all to death, but they can be a nuisance. Lionelle once tried to give a dead mouse to a customer.

Store Owner

Midnite

Clock Repair Shop

Time means nothing to a cat.

Repairman

Mini Cherie

Apparel Design Company

Mini Cherie is a Sagittarius, which makes her extremely independent and self-centered. She's also a Siamese, which gives her a high level of intellect but also means she's very high-strung. I got her as a companion to Cyrus, my Gemini Himalayan.

Designer

82

Anthony Boucher Ink

Mystery Bookshop

People ask—since we sell only mystery books—why we don't have a *black* cat. Well, I think all cats are mysterious—especially once you get to know their personality.

Owner, Murder Ink

85

Moshe

Memorial and Monument Showroom

He's the only cat we've had who has taken up biblical studies.
We first noticed his interest in Hebrew when he was very young
and took to sleeping on the Old Testament.

Stonecutter

Fluffy

Rock Nightclub

The cat and I have been friends
a long time... We both know
things nobody else knows...like
who runs this planet...where
the aliens are landing....

Rocker

89

Unemployed Cat

You want to take that cat's picture? Just take him with you, huh?

Merchant

97

Mary Lou

Foundry

I never liked cats much myself. Always had a dog around the house. I didn't think nothing about it when that cat started hanging around here. But then I started thinking one day about why an animal that didn't have to would live in a place like this. She's always grimy and hungry and wet. I can't afford and don't even want no pet, but every chance I get I bring a little food from home. Ain't no reason for an animal to starve like that.

Machinist

98

Frank

Tire Repair Shop

Frank's the best deal I ever got. Paid just ten dollars for him and I haven't seen a rat since. Heck, I bet he'll be doing good work long after his warranty runs out.

Repairman

Crimson

College Boiler Room

You should see *him* blow off steam.

Engineer

102

Unnamed cats

Steel Mill

I been here thirty-seven years
and there isn't a day I can
remember when we didn't have
cats. We've had as many as
thirty at one time. We make a
collection every couple weeks
for their food. Most guys give a
buck or so. In thirty-seven years
I've never seen a rat. I think we
run one of the biggest
cathouses in Pennsylvania.

Steelworker

Kid Vicious

Punk Shop

Cats survive, man. They use people or they kill other animals.
Know what I mean? Gut-level stuff. I dig them.

Punk Regalia Salesman

Maggie

Penitentiary

Her mother was here when I came—and I've been in a long
time. I won't tell you what for. Anyway, her mother was here
for years—she was the best ratter I ever seen—till she took
sick and died. Now Maggie, she's young yet. She's just learning
the ropes.

Prisoner

Houdini

Humane Society

They've yet to build a cage to hold Houdini.

Humane Society Worker

116

Willie

Firehouse

Every firehouse needs a mascot, and nobody uses Dalmatians these days.

Fireman

J.P.

Stock Exchange

We have a joke in the office
about getting all our tips from
J.P. We even tell some of our
clients that we're neither bullish
nor bearish about the
market—we're cat-ish.

Wall Street Stockbroker

121

Devo

Fraidee is off camera

Radio Station

Meeeeoooowww.... This is rock and roll radio. We've got a couple of furry felines in the booth today and they're having a ball. Aren't ya, fellas? Now here's Al Stewart, 'Year of the Cat.' Yeah....

Disc Jockey

Tiffany *foreground*
Beacon *background*

Broadway Audition

CAT CALL. Is there an aspiring Morris hanging around the house, eating tuna fish and sleeping all day? Would you like to put him, her or it to work to pay for all that food? Well, here's your chance. There's a nice juicy role for a big docile cat in the new musical starring Liv Ullmann, "I Remember Mama." And Monday morning, at 11 a.m., on the main floor of the 1 Times Square building (at 42d St.), there will be an open casting call for the right feline. Producers Alexander H. Cohen and Hildy Parks, and director-lyricist Martin Charnin will be on hand to audition the cats, male or female. Their only stipulation is that the cat cannot be pedigreed and must have an animated tail.

Newspaper Ad

131

Rosencrantz and Guildenstern

Theater

We hired Rosencrantz as Chairman of the Board of
Rodent Control. But his companion, Guildenstern, has stars
in her eyes. What a scene stealer she is!

Director

133

Elmer

Talent Agency

The kid's got a face, you know? I discovered him in Elmer's Restaurant across the street. A natural. He's bound to be a star—you know why? He's got a good agent.

Talent Agent

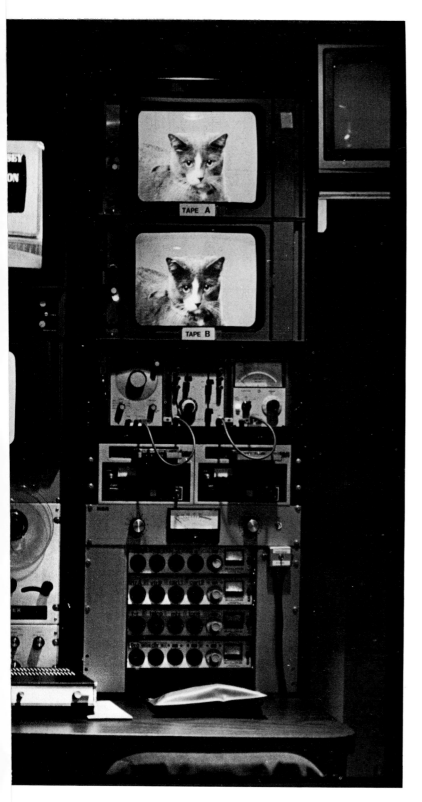

N.J.

Public Television Station

N.J. is public television's Walter Cronkite. He's the best news catter in the business.

Camera Operator

Zinn

Typesetting Firm

It's great having Zinn at the office because she's such good company. She's a talker, but when you work with printed words all day, it's nice to have a conversationalist around.

Typesetter

Macho Man

Data Processing Company

You're welcome to take pictures if you can catch him.

Computer Programmer

Toasty

After Hours Club

He's my silent partner. He prefers to remain behind the scenes.

Owner

Norman

Vegetable Stand

He eats three cans a day. I'd save a lot of money if I could find a vegetarian cat.

Manager

146

Cee

Health Food Store

Cee is the love of my life. I can take her in megadoses.

Cashier

150

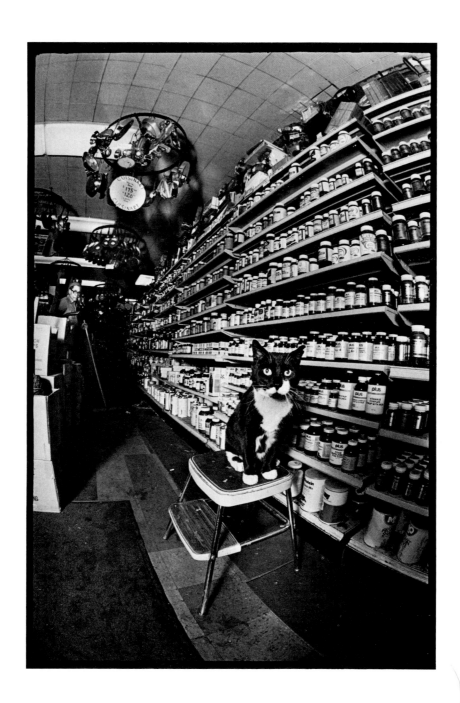

Maraschino Cherry and Misbehavin'

Pornographic Film Company

The only thing pornographic about those cats is their deep-throated purr.

Film Distributor

152

Sibelius

Antiques Store

Sibelius knows his antiques; he only breaks the expensive ones.

Antiques Dealer

155

Louise

Interior Design Company

Cats have had a strong influence on my work. I like warm, simple, organic forms.

Interior Designer

Caesar

Taxidermy Shop

I once kidded the wife about my stuffing Caesar after he passed on, but she didn't take it so good.

Taxidermist

160

Butch

Butcher Shop

We got a deal. He stays off my table and I stay off his tail.

Butcher

Guido

Tool and Die Shop

That cat must think he's some feline Arnold Schwarzenegger
or something. I think I'll put him in a movie and call it
'Pumping Tuna'—or something.

Diemaker

165

Douglas

Shoeshine Shop

That cat found me. I put a sign in the window for the longest time hoping to find his owner, but nothing ever happened. Took him home for a while, but that just didn't work out....Anyway, I brought him here to the shop and he loved it. The customers like him and he loves their attention. He'll leap up into their laps or play with their shoelaces. I've had a lot of offers from people who want to buy him, but I'm going to keep him right here.

Bootblack

166

Gladys

Boutique

I sell clothes to people with originality. My things aren't faddish or trendy, they're unique, individual. That's what kind of people I get in here. So the cat belongs.

Shop Owner

168

Ruba

Italian Restaurant

She's at home here with all of us—except Mrs. Murphy. Ruba ignores her by closing her eyes and pretending to sleep.

Waiter

171

Sheik

Gas Station

When the cat showed up I told my kid he shouldn't count on Sheik hanging around too long. That was six years ago. My kid's now in college.

Station Owner

Author's Note

How do you find a working cat? I began by scouring my neighborhood, store to store, business to business, bar to bar. This uncovered several functioning felines mostly of the grocery genus. I used the yellow pages and called categorically: A for accountants, acoustics, advertising agencies, antiques, automobiles, and azaleas. I ran this ad in several publications:

Does Your Cat Keep Shop? Do You Have a Blue Collar Kitty? Does Your Cat Earn Its Keep? We're looking for cats who live and/or work in *unusual* places like theatres, churches, public and private offices, factories, galleries, schools, etc., to be photographed (no remuneration) for a book by a major publisher. If you know of an agreeable feline purveyor of public relations, a furred floorwalker or any photogenic cat in congenial working surroundings, please call Terry Gruber, LT 1-6470.

The response from all three fronts was tremendous. I was getting calls from all walks of life:

"There's a bar with a Burmese."
"I know a fish store in the Heights with a calico."
"A steel mill in Pennsylvania has twelve cats."

All of a sudden I was up to my ears in cats—cats of all shapes, sizes, colors, kinds, and professions. I would finish one shooting, stop into a smoke shop for gum and see Cleopatra on the Bazooka, photograph her, and go on to the next cat. There were camera-shy cats, showoffs, and cats who tried to come home with me. My camera began to develop hair balls. I had to blow them out twice daily.

Finally, I had to stop and ask myself, "What is this suddenly not-so-rare species called a 'Working Cat'?" Does it really work? The truth is, some do and some don't. Just like people.

Index

175